CLEOPATRA VII
THE LAST PHARAOH OF ANCIENT EGYPT

History Picture Books
Children's Ancient History

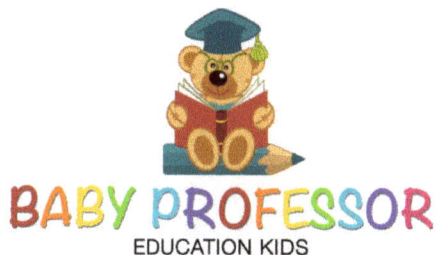

BABY PROFESSOR
EDUCATION KIDS

Speedy Publishing LLC

40 E. Main St. #1156

Newark, DE 19711

www.speedypublishing.com

Copyright 2017

Cleopatra VII was the last Pharaoh of Egypt. She was born in 69 BC and passed away on August 12th in 30 BC. She has been the subject of several plays and movies and plays including the well-known 1963 film that starred Elizabeth Taylor. In this book, you will learn about her life as a Pharaoh.

HISTORY

She was born as a princess of Egypt. Pharaoh Ptolemy XII was her father. She was very cunning and smart while she was growing up. Her father favored her as a child, and she learned from him about how he ruled the country.

Ptolemy XII

Alexander the Great

Her family had been the rulers of Egypt for 300 years. Alexander the Great, the Greek ruler, established the Ptolemy dynasty which included her family. While they were Egyptian rulers, they were from Greece. She was raised writing, speaking and reading Greek. Cleopatra learned several other languages that included Latin and Egyptian.

HER FATHER'S DEATH

At the age of 18, Cleopatra's father passed away, leaving the throne to her and Ptolemy XIII, her younger brother. She married her 10-year-old brother and they became co-rulers of Egypt.

Cleopatra

Cleopatra

Since Cleopatra was so much older, she quickly retained control as Egypt's main ruler. However, her brother desired more power as he got older. He eventually forced her from rule and he took over as Pharaoh.

JULIUS CAESAR

Julius Caesar arrived in 48 BC. Cleopatra was able to sneak inside the palace inside a carpet that was rolled up. Cleopatra talked Caesar into helping her win the throne back. At the battle of the Nile, Caesar was able to defeat Ptolemy's army and while trying to escape, Ptolemy drowned in the Nile River.

Julius Caesar

Cleopatra

Cleopatra then retained power once again. First, she ruled along with Ptolemy XIV, another younger brother, and once he died, she ruled alongside her son Ptolemy Caesarion.

Julius and Cleopatra fell in love and had a child they named Caesarion. Cleopatra went to Rome and lived at one of Caesar's country homes. In spite of her involvement with Caesar, she wanted Egypt to continue to be independent of Rome.

Julius Caesar and Cleopatra

Cleopatra

The economy of Egypt grew under her rule, and trade was established with several Arab nations. Cleopatra became a popular ruler among the Egyptian people since she embraced their culture as well as the country becoming prosperous under her rule.

any people of Rome believed that he held too much power. They worried that his rule would sink the Roman Republic. The people plotted about killing him. Cassius and Brutus were the leaders of this plot. Caesar entered the Senate on March 15, 44 BC. Several men started attacking him and murdered him by stabbing him 23 times.

Caesar's Death

Cleopatra and Octavian

THE ROMAN CIVIL WAR

During this war between the Caesarian faction, Cleopatra sided with the Caesarian party, led by Octavian and Marc Antony, and the faction which included Caesar's assassins that were led by Gaius Cassius Longinus and Marcus Junius Brutus.

Cassius and Brutus left Italy to go east of the Roman Empire, where they were able to conquer established military bases and large areas. Cleopatra then formed an alliance in 43 BC with the Caesarian party of the east, Publius Cornelius Dolabella, who recognized her co-ruler, Caesarion. However, Dolabella soon became encircled and committed suicide in Laodicea.

Laodicea

Dolabella

Cassius hoped to invade Egypt and seize that country's treasures and punish Cleopatra because of her support of Dolabella. Since Egypt did not have strong forces and there was an epidemic and famine, it seemed like an easy target.

He also hoped to stop Cleopatra from adding reinforcements for Octavian and Antony. He was not able to execute the invasion as Brutus summoned him to return to Smyrna toward the end of 43 BC. Cassius attempted to block her route towards the Caesarians.

Cleopatra and Antony

In order to do this, Lucius Staius Murcus moved along with 60 ships in addition to elite troops south of the Peloponnese at Matapan. However, Cleopatra was able to sail along with her fleet from Alexandria towards the west along the coast of Libya in order to meet the Caesarian leaders, but was forced to return to Egypt since a violent storm damaged her ships and she also became ill. Murcus learned about her misfortune and found wreckage of her ships near the coast of Greece. He proceeded to sail with his ships towards the Adriatic Sea.

WHO WAS MARC ANTONY?

Caesar was assassinated in 44 BC, and Cleopatra decided to return to Egypt. Marc Antony was one of three leaders that emerged in Rome after Caesar's death. Cleopatra met Marc Antony and they fell in love in 41 BC. They created a military alliance against Octavian, another one of Rome's leaders.

Meeting of Marc Antony and Cleopatra

Julius Caesar's legal heir was Octavian. Cleopatra felt that her son, Caesarion, should be his heir and eventually become Rome's ruler. She felt that Antony could help her with this goal.

Battle of Actium

Camp of Octavian

Nicopolis

T. Taurus

Ambracian Gulf

M. Agrippa

L. Publicola
M. Antonius

L. Arruntius

M. Octavius
M. Insteius

Cleopatra

Actium

P. Canidius

Camp of Mark Antony

Anactorium

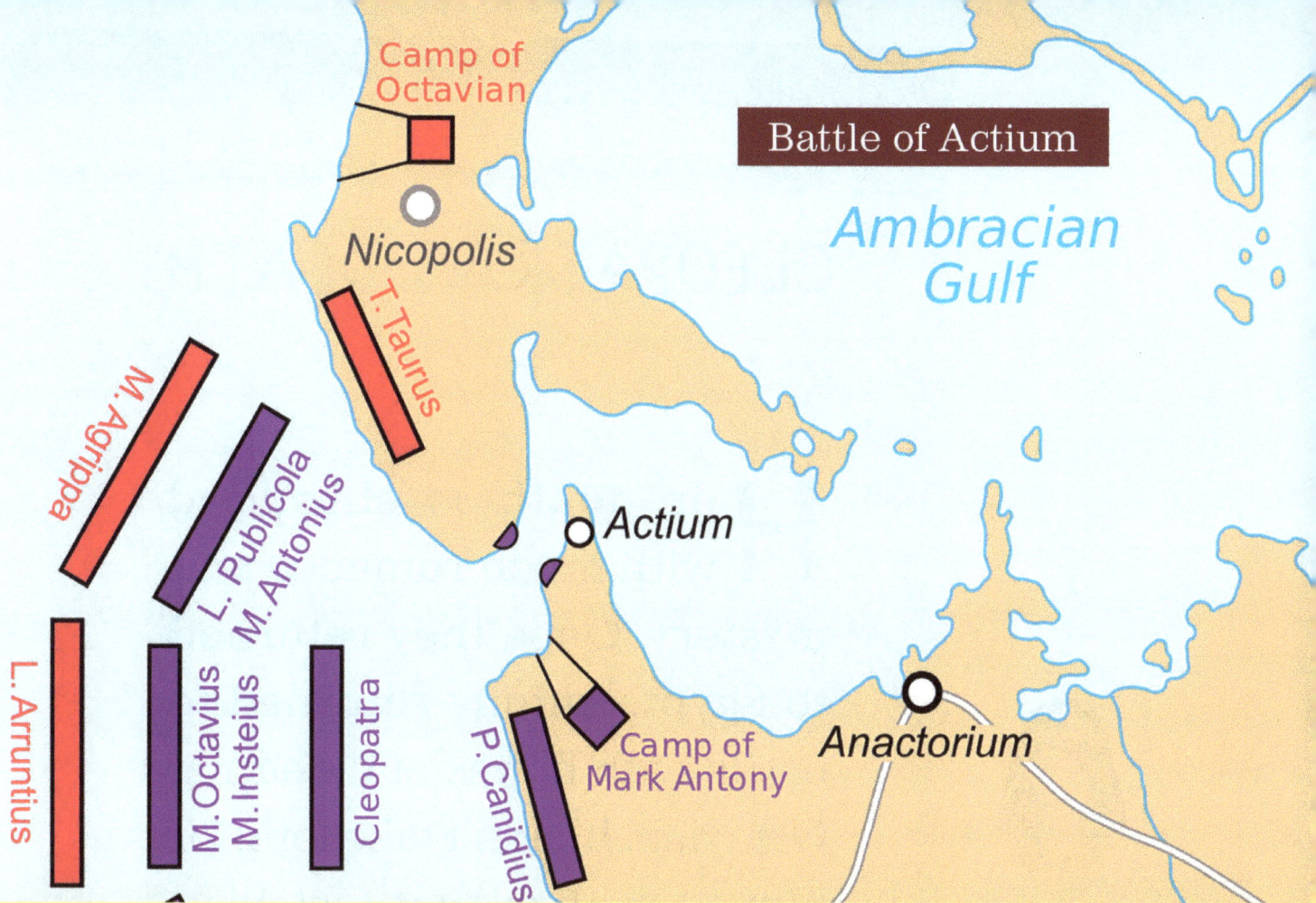

Marc and Cleopatra merged their armies to fight Octavian and these forces met during the Battle of Actium. They lost to Octavian and retreated to Egypt.

CLEOPATRA'S DEATH

Her death is shrouded with much romance and mystery. Once they returned to Egypt, Antony returned to battle with hopes of defeating Octavian. It didn't take long for him to realize that Octavian was going to capture him. When he heard the false news of Cleopatra's death, he killed himself.

Death of Cleopatra

Cleopatra became very sad hearing of Antony's death. She proceeded to kill herself, allowing a poisonous cobra to bite her. After her death, Octavian took over control of Egypt and Egypt then became a part of the Roman Empire. Cleopatra's death caused the end of the Ptolemy dynasty as well as the Egyptian Empire. She then became the last Pharaoh of Egypt.

PHARAOHS

The supreme leaders of the land were the Pharaohs of Ancient Egypt, similar to emperors or kings. They ruled over both lower and upper Egypt and were both the religious and political leaders. They were often referred to as a god.

Pharaoh

The word Pharaoh comes from the word meaning "great house", which describes a kingdom or palace. The wife of the Pharaoh, otherwise known as the Queen of Egypt, were considered to be powerful rulers as well. Women would become rulers occasionally and were called Pharaoh, but typically it would be a man. The current Pharaoh's son would inherit the title and often go through the training so that he would be a great leader.

Historians have divided the timeline of the history of Ancient Egypt by dynasties of the Pharaohs. When one family maintained power, and handed the throne down to an heir, this was known as a dynasty. Generally, there are known to be 31 dynasties during the 3000 years of the history of Ancient Egypt.

Ancient Egypt

Tutankhamun Mask

Throughout Ancient Egypt's history, there were several great Pharaohs. Some of the more famous ones are Akhenaten, Tutankhamun, Hatshepsut, Amenhotep III, Ramses II, and, of course, Cleopatra VII.

THE GOVERNMENT OF ANCIENT EGYPT

Ancient Egypt Government was ruled by the Pharaoh first and foremost. Not only was the Pharaoh the supreme leader of the government, but also ruled over religion. The Pharaoh could not run this government by himself, however, and had a hierarchy of leaders and rulers under him to run the different aspects of this government.

Pharaoh

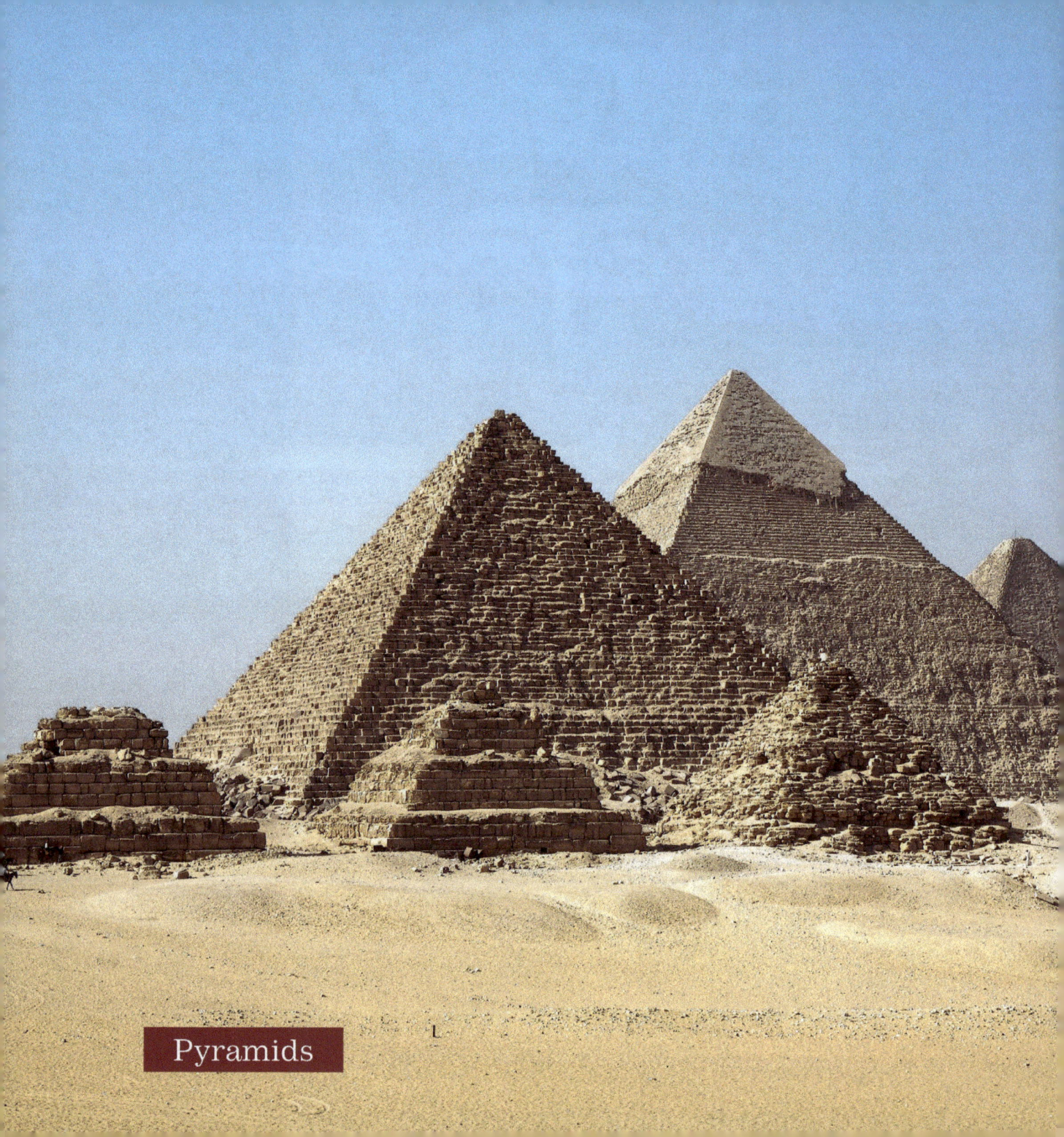

Pyramids

VIZIER

The Vizier was the Primary leader beneath the Pharaoh and was the Chief Overseer of the land, similar to a Prime Minister. The other officers reported to the vizier. Imhotep was possibly the most well-known vizier. He was the architect of the original pyramid and later was made into a god.

NOMARKS

Local governors below the vizier were known as Nomarks. They would rule over a section of land referred to as a nome, which was similar to a province or state. The Pharaoh would sometimes appoint the nomarks, but occasionally this position might be heredity and handed from a father to a son.

OTHER OFFICIALS

The minister of public works, the chief treasurer, and the army commander were other officials that would report to the Pharaoh. Each of these officials had separate powers and responsibilities, however, the Pharaoh would have the final word. Many of these officials were scribes and priests.

Important to the government, the scribes recorded taxes and census, as well as managing finances. The overseers of the lands also were appointed and kept track of farms and ensure they were performing their jobs.

MONARCHY

An average person would have no say. However, since the Pharaoh was referred to as a god, as well as the people's representative to the gods, often they would accept the Pharaoh as the supreme leader with no complaints.

There is so much more to learn about Cleopatra, Ancient Egypt, and the Pharaohs. For additional information, you can go to your local library, research the internet, and ask questions of your teachers, family and friends. You may also want to ask your parents about watching one of the movies made about her life.